"Fatherlessness is the most detrimental and far-reaching issue on the planet. Virtually every social ill in our urban communities (gang involvement, drug and alcohol abuse, crime, violence, poverty, etc.) can be traced back to the effects of abandonment and a father-wound. Peter Watts, who is one of my heroes, has been on a thirty-year journey toward healing and overcoming the effects of an absent father. He is breaking the chain of abandonment by being a faithful and committed husband to his wife, and a loving and engaged father to his children."
 —DR. LARRY ACOSTA, president and founder
 of the Urban Youth Workers Institute

"Peter Watts' faith, integrity, and most importantly life experience, makes him the perfect man to address an issue that is killing America—rampant fatherlessness. As someone who was once abandoned by his dad, he has the compassion and understanding to speak to those with similar stories. As a pastor and loving dad, he offers wisdom to fathers who are fulfilling their duties; and to those who are not, he offers hope."
 —CHRIS BROUSSARD, Fox Sports

"There isn't a relationship I value more than the one I have with my father. I realize that I am fortunate to have a father who is living and involved. He not only

PRAISE FOR *PRODIGAL FATHER*

shared with me his build, his personality, and his general disposition; but he also shared with me his time. My father's presence helped me discover the breadth of my potential, and the limits of who I could be. The value and prophetic destiny of my last name means the world to me. I had a natural father who saw it as his duty by God to think generationally. Pastor Peter's journey unlocks the importance that fathering means to us all. I thank him for sharing his journey, and I recommend it to all readers!"
—PASTOR TERRELL FLETCHER, author, speaker

Prodigal Father
Peter Watts, Jr.

© 2017 Peter Watts, Jr.

All rights reserved. No part of this book may be reproduced or transmitted in any form or by any means, electronic or mechanical, including photocopying, recording, or by any information storage and retrieval system, without written permission from the author, except for the inclusion of brief quotations in a review.

Published in Los Angeles, California, by Chontali Kirk Books.

Cover design by Robert Kirk.

Unless otherwise noted, Scripture quotations are from the ESV® Bible (The Holy Bible, English Standard Version®), copyright © 2001 by Crossway, a publishing ministry of Good News Publishers. Used by permission. All rights reserved.

Prodigal Father may be purchased in bulk for educational, business, fundraising, or sales promotional use. For information, please contact:

Peter Watts, Jr.
http://www.peterwattsjr.com
http://therockchurch2020vision.blogspot.com/
1613 W. 20th Street
Los Angeles, CA 90007
(424) 372-7625

ISBN: 978-1975656737
Printed in the USA

This book is dedicated to my mother. She is a strong woman of God with a deep faith that keeps her grounded. She never tried to play the role of being a father to me. She has been a mother who has loved, cared, supported, and challenged me in every phase of my life. She raised my younger sister and me, and oftentimes sacrificed her needs to ensure that we had everything we needed. She embodies the Proverbs 31 passage, which says, "Honor her for all that her hands have done, and let her works bring her praise **at the city gate.**"

(v. 31, NIV)

Contents

Foreword...... ix
Oh Father, Where Art Thou?...... xiii
Introduction...... xv

Chapter 1: Fatherless Generation...... 1
Chapter 2: A Father Forever...... 7
Chapter 3: When Did I See You Hungry?...... 17
Chapter 4: Prodigal Father...... 21
Chapter 5: Mercy...... 27
Chapter 6: Baggage In Marriage...... 31
Chapter 7: Who's Ya Daddy?...... 35
Chapter 8: Teacher/Principal/Pastor/Friend...... 45
Chapter 9: Letter To My Younger Self...... 55
Chapter 10: Make Your Pain Count...... 59
Chapter 11: My Mother's Perspective...... 69
Chapter 12: For*grieve*ness...... 85

Notes...... 93

Foreword

"Use the pain of your story to leverage your relationship with youth."

—**Rev. Dr. Efrem Smith, co-lead pastor; Bayside Church, Midtown; and author of *Killing Us Softly***

The abandonment or loss of a father can have a significant impact on a person's journey from childhood to adulthood. For the African American male, there are unique challenges to be navigated. There are some, who are both politically conservative and theologically evangelical, who believe the absence of Fathers is the major reason for the negative issues plaguing predominately under-resourced, African American communities. These issues include gang violence, drug selling/addiction, and questionable fashion statements, to name a few. Other social elements such as institutional racism, the targeting of such communities by alcohol and tobacco companies, abandonment by large businesses and banks, and a lack of serious criminal justice reform, are ignored as contributors to the state of predominately under-resourced, African American communities.

FOREWORD

Regardless of the opinions on root causes, there are too many African American males growing up without fathers present to walk with them into manhood. I encourage those who believe that this is just an issue for the African American community to fix, to reflect for a moment on the history of Black people in this country. During slavery, the Black family was unrecognized and overwhelmed by trauma. Black families were often split up through the selling of children and spouses, and in some cases Black men had to watch their wives being raped by slave masters.

This tragic time in American history was followed up by Jim Crow segregation throughout the Southern states. Many African American men left their families in the South and headed North, hoping to find better paying jobs that would afford them the opportunity to send for their families to rejoin them at some point. Though many African American males served bravely in the military, they were not provided the same opportunities at home ownership and education as their White male counterparts. In too many cases, they returned from war to drug infested and poverty-stricken communities—nothing close to a hero's welcome. One could argue that any form of a significant family structure for African Americans is a miracle of sorts, when you thoroughly survey the historic and systemic odds that have been faced.

FOREWORD

The African American Church, which was birthed in the midst of slavery and White supremacy, has been a liberating, reconciling, transformative, and empowering force in spite of the odds stacked against Black people. It has been a laboratory of leadership development, a sanctuary pointing to salvation in Christ, and collectively a dynamic movement for social change. The African American Church has been an outpost of the Kingdom of God within the context of the journey of Black people, addressing both individual responsibility (you must be born again) and systemic oppression (we must demand our freedom). Both revival and revolution has been the true task of the African American Church. To abandon these elements is to remove the identity and soul of the African American Church.

I lift up this larger narrative of African American people, because it will help bring a deeper understanding to the individual story of Pastor Peter Watts. His story is one glimpse into the struggles, pain, dreams, victories, and transformation that takes place within the challenging and complex journey of a people still seeking full access and acceptance into the fabric of the American dream and promise. I have had the privilege of serving in ministry with Pastor Watts. I have also shared moments of laughter over catfish and fries, and moments of grief over too many unarmed African Americans losing their lives without a deep dive into police and criminal justice reform. I have been blessed through an up-close connection with him, and I hope you will be blessed by his powerful journey.

—Rev. Dr. Efrem Smith,
Bayside Church, Midtown

Oh Father, Where Art Thou?

Growing up in inner city Los Angeles, a young man could find himself in an interesting paradox. He could be fatherless and at the same time surrounded by fathers. He would just call them by different names. When I was younger, I called them *Big Homies*, *OGs*, *Uncles*, and sometimes the very city itself. It wasn't so much that my Pops wasn't around. It was that I was drowning in dads, and at the end of the day, I just wanted my own.

Had I read about my Dad in a book, I would consider him my hero. He was a Black Panther, a Vietnam war vet, had a full ride to Arizona State for basketball before those draft papers came. He split with Mom when I was fourteen.

It's not so much that my Dad wasn't present. He just was not the man I fancied him to be. He was, in fact, just a man. Not a hero, not villain. Just a man.

He was a man who probably suffered from PTSD, either from the war or the Jim Crow South. Either way, the sixties, the war on drugs, racial injustice, womanizing, and his own father being absent, robbed me of having the Dad I wished for. He did his best. I don't hate him. I love him dearly, and our relationship is great now. But I have many regrets.

I regret that it was Alex Carassco—not my father—who taught me how to change the oil. It was Jr. Martinez, a neighbor down the street, who told me what sex was. I regret having to listen to Marcus Jones' advice on how to deal with the Piru bloods, since my Dad was too busy to take the time to give me this advice.

On the other hand, I can't be more grateful for the men who filled in the gaps. We all have blind spots, and God didn't allow me to suffer because of my Dad. I just hope God does the same for my daughters.

—Propaganda,
Rapper, Pastor, Poet

Introduction

I've been in ministry for over twenty years. I was saved and baptized when I was a young child in elementary school. Throughout my years in the local church, I have heard the story of the prodigal son preached a lot.

This particular parable is one of many found in the gospel of Luke, and it is used to demonstrate characteristics of the Kingdom of God. In this parable, Jesus tells of a father who had two sons. The younger son came to the father and asked for his inheritance. The father obliged him, and divided his wealth between his two sons. As described in Luke 15, the younger son received what was due to him, and carelessly wasted all of his money on wild partying.

> Not many days later, the younger son gathered all he had and took a journey into a far country, and there he squandered his property in reckless living. (v. 13)

After more days had passed, a famine came upon the land, and the son found himself in extreme need. He had no money, no place to live, and no family to depend on. He hired himself out as a last resort, and found himself in a pigpen

INTRODUCTION

eating the same slop on which the pigs feasted. The pivotal point in this text is when the son realized he was not living the life God designed and purposed for him. The text states:

> But when he came to himself, he said, "How many of my father's hired servants have more than enough bread, but I perish here with hunger! I will arise and go to my father, and I will say to him, 'Father, I have sinned against heaven and before you. I am no longer worthy to be called your son. Treat me as one of your hired servants.'" And he arose and came to his father. (v. 17-20)

The most important part of this parable was that the son came to himself. He realized the life he was living wasn't sustainable. He realized what he had under his father's roof was much better than what the world had to offer. As a result, he returned home in hopes of being received by his father. Surprisingly, the father greeted him with open arms. With compassion in his heart, the father ran toward his son in the middle of the road and embraced him with a kiss, demonstrating that all was forgiven.

In my case, the tables were turned. My *dad* decided to leave and squander his life in wild living. He found himself homeless, and eating slop and other people's unwanted food from trashcans. My father became the son, and I took on the role of the father. I was the one who had to demonstrate

INTRODUCTION

compassion toward him, even though he was willing to risk jeopardizing the stability of his family. It was only by the grace of God that we were united, but more importantly, that I was able to forgive him instantly when I saw him *coming up the road.*

Growing up, I often wondered what it would be like to forgive someone, even if they didn't deserve it. That's when I began this journey of the *prodigal father.* The relationship between a father and son is important, but there are so many children growing up without their fathers. In the United States, the percentage of children living without their biological fathers in the home are staggering[1]:

57.6 percent of black children
31.2 percent of Hispanic children
20.7 percent of white children

I decided to write this book and share my story in hopes of helping others who grew up without a father. This country is filled with people facing challenges due to old father wounds. As a result, they suffer from resentment, anger, low self-esteem and unforgiveness.

This book is also for fathers who don't have relationships with their biological children. There are many fathers who would love to see their kids, but they believe in the lies about their own lives, which keep them from pursuing reconciliation.

INTRODUCTION

As you read my story, I pray you are challenged to begin a journey of restoration and reuniting with your own father, son, or daughter. This doesn't mean that all problems will be fixed in an instant. What it does mean, however, is that all the hurt and pain caused by your past can be healed, and you can be restored. God has a purpose for your life, but to walk in that purpose, your father wounds must be healed.

Chapter 1

FATHERLESS GENERATION

Lately, I have been wrestling with an issue that has haunted me my whole life: fatherlessness. Last week, I attended a workshop called, "A Fatherless Generation," put on by World Impact's former President and CEO Efrem Smith. In that workshop, the one sentence I walked away with was, "Use the pain of your story to leverage your relationship with youth."

Recently, this issue of fatherlessness reared its ugly head again after I viewed a disturbing video on my Facebook feed. The video showed a police officer wrestling a homeless man to the ground and eventually shooting him five times, right in front of The Union Rescue Mission (URM), which is a Christian recovery place for the homeless on Skid Row. As a human being, a civilian, and a black man, this incident disturbed me deeply. But it also brought Efrem's words to mind, *Use your pain.* Hearing about this incident deepened my pain, and compelled me to share my story.

I was born and raised in the greater Los Angeles area. I lived in a two-parent home during my early elementary school years. My father was my hero. He was an entrepreneur and owned his own roofing company. It was a very successful business that he created from the ground up with only a high school education. We were a model family in the community, and everyone knew who we were. However, one summer, things began to change. My dad started coming home later. He and my mom would argue a lot. I would see him drinking more often than normal.

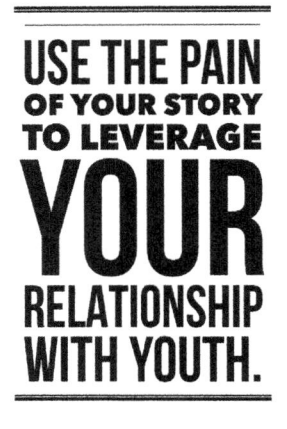

> USE THE PAIN OF YOUR STORY TO LEVERAGE YOUR RELATIONSHIP WITH YOUTH.

When I transitioned to the third grade, my mom decided to leave my dad, and we had to go live with my grandparents. When I asked my mom why we were leaving, she said, with tears in her eyes, "Your daddy started using heroin and he is very abusive to me. I want our family to be safe." As an 8-year-old kid, I couldn't grasp the fact that I would no longer be living with my dad.

Throughout my elementary school years, my dad would come to visit me at my grandparents' house, but oftentimes he would come under the influence of drugs and alcohol and would not be allowed to see me. I can vividly remember my dad arguing and fighting with my grandfather in the backyard. My grandfather didn't want my dad to try and kidnap me at gunpoint, as he had done before.

As a child, the last contact I had with my dad was over the phone when he promised to send me a fifty-dollar allowance. I still remember going to the mailbox everyday when I got out of school to look for a check or cash from my dad, but unfortunately it never came.

When I became an adult, I had already settled in my heart that my dad was no longer a part of my life, and I had to move on. In the spring of 2003, my uncle, who was a sanitation worker, came over my house and told me he had seen my father on Skid Row. My uncle wondered if I wanted to go see him and offered to take me. At this time in my life, I had been married for nine years with three small children. I thought about it and said, "Yes, I would love to see Peter Watts, Sr." In my heart, I wanted to see him because I had so much anger toward him and wanted to let him know how much he had hurt me.

I drove down to Skid Row with my wife and kids, hoping to find this man. I wanted to give him a piece of my mind and show him the family he

> **IN MY HEART, I WANTED TO SEE HIM BECAUSE I HAD SO MUCH ANGER TOWARD HIM AND WANTED TO LET HIM KNOW HOW MUCH HE HAD HURT ME.**

had missed out on. As I drove down the street, I saw him wearing filthy clothes and pushing a shopping cart into the local liquor store. I pulled over my car, jumped out, and stood outside of the store waiting for him to come out. After five minutes had gone by, he came out of the store and we looked at each other face-to-face. When I thought I was at last ready to unload the hurt and pain that had built up over the past 29 years, a spirit of forgiveness came over me. We locked eyes. He began to cry and so did I. We embraced for what seemed like hours as he repeatedly said, "I'm sorry for what I did to you and your mom."

> **WE EMBRACED FOR WHAT SEEMED LIKE HOURS AS HE REPEATEDLY SAID, "I'M SORRY FOR WHAT I DID TO YOU AND YOUR MOM."**

I tried to build a new relationship with him, but unfortunately we lost touch again and I hadn't seen him since. Seeing the video of a black male on Skid Row being shot and killed by the hands of law enforcement brought back these feelings of guilt and frustration. I think what hurt me the most was the fact that, at that time, they didn't have a picture or the birth name of the man. All they released was his street name, "Africa." All I could think to myself was, *What if that were my father?*

I have had a chance to process my feelings and think about what I need to share with the world. I have come to the conclusion that God has me at World Impact to, in the words of Efrem, *leverage this pain*. What if my father—who is part of the urban poor, the marginalized, and the forgotten in the city—had been empowered by the Gospel? What if my father had been a TUMI[2] graduate or lived in a SIAFU[3] Leadership home where he would have been mentored and trained for the work of the ministry? I will always have to live with this thorn in my flesh, but I also hear the voice of Christ speaking to me, "My grace is sufficient."

Chapter 2

A FATHER FOREVER

Two weeks ago, I was as close to the edge as one can be. Close to prison. Close to death. Bills and responsibilities chased me. My strength was fading. My focus was blurred and my faith had withered. I felt as if I were in a tornado. I cried out to God for help. Pastor Peter Watts heard my pain and financially covered my way to the SIAFU Men's Retreat.

As we ate breakfast, tears of gratefulness flowed from my eyes. No one knew that on the previous day, I had planned to acquire a weapon to seek revenge on my enemy. It is nothing short of amazing to be one day suffering in a storm, and the next day eating with powerful men of God on the mountaintop. I had so much anger and resentment in my heart, but all of it melted away at the retreat. I was transformed on that mountain at the Oaks.

After returning from the SIAFU Men's Retreat, I have increased my fellowship with the men's group at The Rock Church. I feel truly blessed to be surrounded by humble, powerful men of God. I'm reminded of the scripture that states, "A man's gift makes room for him and brings him before the great" (Prov. 18:16).

—Coach Lou

PRODIGAL FATHER

This is the testimony of Coach Luis Clarke, also known as Coach Lou. I've come to know him over the years while spending time at the local middle school where my wife was principal. He provided mentorship and uniforms to the students there. I'm humbled by his story, because it is not uncommon to hear men of color speak about their experiences of giving their lives to the Lord after having run the streets for so long.

Coach Lou was born and bred in South Los Angeles. He went to the local high school, and because of unfortunate circumstances, he found himself behind bars as a juvenile. While locked behind bars, he gave his life to the Lord and has been serving God ever since. This doesn't mean his life has become a bed of roses. He still has to overcome the struggles, disappointments, and challenges he inherited as a result of being one of the many returning citizens in our under-resourced community.

I'm humbled that God would use me to spiritually father Coach. He is much older than I am, as are a lot of the men in our church. It feels strange to take on the role of a father in that sense, because I still wrestle with my own father wounds. It is within this context that I have realized the need for pastors and church planters to be fathers. We have enough mentors. We have mentoring programs all over the country. There is the Boys &

Girls Club, Mentors Across America, 100 Black Men, and so many others; but we need more leaders to be fathers.

I've discovered that a mentor is one who points out and guides you to your areas of weakness and lack, but a father is one who comes alongside you to help you grow. Many of our men in the city never had a chance to be raised by our fathers in a healthy environment. Many of us had to learn from a single mother or from the school of hard knocks. The SIAFU Men's Retreat challenges me to be a father in the lives of men. I envision doing this the same way Paul illustrates in 1 Corinthians 4:

> **I'VE DISCOVERED THAT A MENTOR IS ONE WHO POINTS OUT AND GUIDES YOU TO YOUR AREAS OF WEAKNESS AND LACK, BUT A FATHER IS ONE WHO COMES ALONGSIDE YOU TO HELP YOU GROW.**

> For though you have countless guides [or mentors] in Christ, you do not have many fathers. For I became your father in Christ Jesus through the gospel. I urge you, then, be imitators of me. (v. 15-16)

Paul instructs us to lead by example, so those whom we father can follow. I may not be an earthly father to the men in my life, but I've been given the mantle to father them through the gospel of Jesus Christ.

There have been so many men I've had the opportunity to do life with. One in particular that I've had at least thirteen years with is my friend and brother who passed away, Daryl Hadley. Daryl and I met because I taught both of his daughters in elementary school and eventually became their principal once they reached middle school. Daryl was a fun loving man who had a great testimony of transformation and rehabilitation. When I met Daryl, we instantly became friends. Our daughters Imani and Alexandria became best friends from the time they met while in kindergarten at View Park Elementary School. Daryl was much older than I. He could have been an older brother or even a father based on our age difference. Daryl had experienced life as a kid of the sixties, and he was also a Navy veteran. He lived in the Bay Area for a while, before returning to his hometown in Los Angeles. The uniqueness of our relationship had to do with the fact that I not only became his friend, but I also became his pastor and spiritual father in the ministry. Although Daryl had a lot of wisdom from the streets and life in general, God gave me the ability to lead him in spiritual matters of the heart and soul. When life's deep issues would surround him, I was there to be a voice of reason and understanding in his personal life. He shared with me openly his joys and pains, as well as his victories and struggles. One of the things I learned through our relationship was that age doesn't determine whether or not God will use one as a father figure for others. It was evident by our relationship. There were many times when Daryl came to me with questions that only a father could answer. I was honored to be that person in his life on a spiritual level.

I watched Daryl learn how to be a good father to his own children through the relationship he and I developed over the years. Had I functioned as a mentor to Daryl, I don't think the growth in his life would have happened as it did.

As a mentor, I would have played a different role. My role would have been one of correction and direction versus nurturing growth spiritually and emotionally. Mentioned in this chapter is the verse in 1 Corinthians where Paul tells the church to imitate him as he imitated Christ. That's what a good father does. Paul didn't address the church as a teacher in that moment. He came to them as a father would come to his child. He came to the church at Corinth, encouraging them to follow him as he followed Christ.

We are all imitators of something, and we are all influenced by a number of things. Paul insists that if the church is going to mature, it has to imitate the one being followed, which is Christ.

That's what it means to be a father. It's living your life in a way that can be imitated by others. The only way we will be able to lead those who follow us is by following something bigger than ourselves. If you didn't grow up with a father, it is still possible to find a positive model for you to imitate. If you are in spaces and places with people who grew up fatherless, then maybe God is challenging you to be the father they so desperately need. Whether we as men like it or not, we are going to be fathers forever. This includes being a father to our own children, to the ones who live on our block, to those who attend our churches, and to those on the sports teams we happen to coach.

IMITATE CHRIST'S LOVE

What does imitation look like when it comes to following Christ as others follow you? First, it is imitating the way Christ loved others. We see evidence all throughout the gospels where Jesus loved the undesirables according to the standards of this world. He healed lepers and all those society wanted to stay away from. He gave living water to a woman at the well who had been sleeping around with several men. He healed demon-possessed people who had been tormented for years. He fed hungry people who needed nourishment. Ultimately, Jesus gave up His life as a ransom for many, because of His unending love for us. As fathers forever, we must be willing to love those whom God has placed on our paths, even if it seems like they don't deserve it. I've sat in many workshops as an educator and church planter, and the one issue that always comes to the surface regarding youth is that they don't experience enough unconditional love in their lives. When they become adults, most of the troublesome things they do is a response to never being loved by someone who expected nothing in return.

> **ULTIMATELY, JESUS GAVE UP HIS LIFE AS A RANSOM FOR MANY, BECAUSE OF HIS UNENDING LOVE FOR US.**
>
> **AS FATHERS FOREVER, WE MUST BE WILLING** TO LOVE THOSE WHOM GOD HAS PLACED ON **OUR PATHS, EVEN IF IT SEEMS LIKE THEY DON'T DESERVE IT.**

IMITATE CHRIST'S SELFLESSNESS

Another characteristic of Christ that we should imitate is His selflessness. Christ was never about himself or his own comfort. He came as a response to man's sin. When he looked over into the city of Jerusalem, the Bible says he was moved with compassion. It's that compassion that drove him to consider the needs of others. As a father forever, one must be driven by compassion. There has to be something within us that drives us to do for others before we even think of doing for ourselves. I can't count the number of times this rang true in dealing with my own children. On many occasions, I've sacrificed my own needs to ensure that my children had what they needed. We should imitate Christ's compassion and selflessness, when it comes to fathering others.

Below is a poem I read some time ago that speaks directly to the thought of imitating one another:

When God Created Fathers
By Erma Bombeck

When the good Lord was creating fathers,
He started with a tall frame.
A female angel nearby said, "What kind of
father is that? If you're going to make
children so close to the ground, why have
you put fathers up so high? He won't be able
to shoot marbles without kneeling, tuck a
child in bed without bending or even kiss a
child without a lot of stooping."

...And God smiled and said, "Yes, but if I make him child-

A FATHER FOREVER

size, who would children have to look up to?"

At the end of the day, it doesn't matter what kind of father my own father was to me. Ultimately, I have the responsibility of imitating a Father who is trustworthy and never failing. As men, let us always remember to imitate the way Christ loved others, and show selflessness to those in our care. If we stay focused on that, we can be fathers forever.

Chapter 3

WHEN DID I SEE YOU HUNGRY?

The Urban Church Association (UCA) is one of World Impact's national initiatives. When I was asked to lead our UCA in Los Angeles, one of the goals I made was to ensure that churches were connected and working together for the good of the Kingdom. We engage in what my church calls *Impact Sunday.*

Impact Sunday is a day to serve in your local community, and it occurs every fifth Sunday of the month. In January of 2017, we had an opportunity to serve alongside one of our UCA partners and current student at The Urban Ministry Institute (TUMI), Jennifer Chou. Jennifer launched a ministry called *Jesus Knows My Name,* where she is lead pastor. Her ministry serves the homeless community. Each week, Jennifer sets up church in the parking lot of a mechanic shop on Skid Row. Her ministry is to serve food, give away clothes, and conduct worship and prayer sessions for hundreds of men and women who come to be filled physically and spiritually.

On this particular Sunday, a couple of our UCA

ministries shut down our churches (Chosen Generation and The Rock), and came to serve with Jennifer on Skid Row.

Earlier in this book, I shared my story about my own father who lives on Skid Row, and how I haven't seen him in over twenty years. On this particular Sunday, I prayed that I would run into him as I served with Jennifer's ministry. I went downtown to Skid Row, expecting to be a blessing by serving food, and praying for those in need. What I ended up experiencing was something completely different.

I was standing in front of a table that had a large pot of beans, chicken, and broth that we poured into the bowls of each person who came by. This was the first time I remember serving on Skid Row while intently looking into the eyes of every black male that came by, because I was expecting to see my own father. As a result, I ended up having deep conversations with men I would have never had the chance to interact with. I got to know *Eddie*, who was intelligent and surprisingly hilarious. I expected him to be down and out because he lived on the streets, but there

> **I WENT DOWNTOWN TO SKID ROW, EXPECTING TO BE A BLESSING BY SERVING FOOD, AND PRAYING FOR THOSE IN NEED.**
>
> **WHAT I ENDED UP EXPERIENCING WAS SOMETHING COMPLETELY DIFFERENT.**

was something about the joy he had and his free-living nature that I could not grasp or understand. Eddie and I talked and laughed for about an hour that day.

Our ministry served with Jennifer's for about two hours. I drove home with my heart full from meeting so many incredible people. Later, I received an email from Jennifer stating she had heard my story about my father. She explained that she felt compelled by the Holy Spirit to help me find him.

I responded with such gratefulness for her obedience to the Spirit in this situation. Later in the day, Jennifer sent me another email, stating that she had been telling the Skid Row residents about my father. They had decided to come together as a homeless community and help me find my father! To think I went to the homeless community expecting to bless others; but in God's wisdom, I ended up being the recipient of His grace in ways I didn't expect.

> **THIS WAS THE FIRST TIME I REMEMBER SERVING ON SKID ROW WHILE INTENTLY LOOKING INTO THE EYES OF EVERY BLACK MALE THAT CAME BY, BECAUSE I WAS EXPECTING TO SEE MY OWN FATHER.**

I thought Matthew 25 was Jesus' instructions on how to help those less fortunate, but little did I know that I was one of those He spoke of.

> Truly, I say to you, as you did not do it to one of the least of these, you did not do it to Me. (v. 45)

Chapter 4

PRODIGAL FATHER

If you have been following me or my blog posts, I'm sure you are well aware of my father wounds. I have written about my father who hasn't been in my life since the second grade. Now, I'm 44 years old, and it has been over thirty years since I've seen him. Not having a father in your life brings about some internal and emotional issues that only God can heal. We often read in the gospels about the parable of the prodigal or wayward son. What happens when you have a prodigal *father* who has left his family looking for what he thinks is a better life? Well, let me share with you my story of redemption with added details.

    I grew up in a two-parent household until I was in the second grade. My father was my world. He was a business owner and entrepreneur. He had his own roofing company and supported my mother, my younger sister, and me. He was a bright man—highly intelligent and had an impeccable ability to memorize things. I remember a time when he had to go to court over a contract issue against a large corporation; he represented himself. Needless to say, he won the case on his own. That's how intelligent he was.

In the early seventies, families in the black community were falling apart. Drugs hit the scene, and people were experimenting with them and getting hooked. My family was no exception. My dad started using drugs and had gotten hooked. He began exhibiting behaviors of violence and instability that my mother would not tolerate. She gathered her strength, and took my sister and me to Los Angeles where we lived with my grandparents.

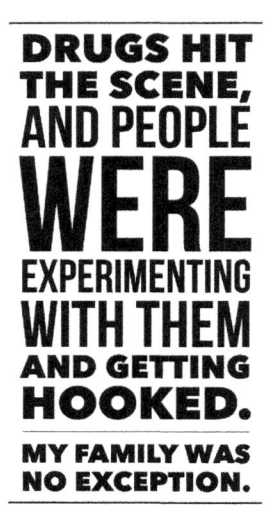

> **DRUGS HIT THE SCENE, AND PEOPLE WERE EXPERIMENTING WITH THEM AND GETTING HOOKED. MY FAMILY WAS NO EXCEPTION.**

As mentioned earlier, I had little contact with my father during my elementary school years. His visits were brief, and he would often show up to the house high on *sherm*.[4] Sometimes he would literally pull out a gun on my mother and kidnap me and take me to his house in Inglewood. After he would come down from his high, he would be regretful and take me back home to my mother. I was traumatized by these events, which happened on more than one occasion. Soon he stopped coming by and stopped calling altogether. I was in the fourth grade when I last had contact with him. His last words to me were, "I'm going to send you money each month."

As a kid, I believed him. Each day, when I arrived home from school, I would go to the mailbox expecting to see an envelope with an allowance inside. But there would be nothing inside. Eventually, I gave up on my dad and moved forward in my life.

During these formative years, it was my grandfather, uncles, and football coach who became the father figures I so desperately needed to help me mature. Once I graduated from high school and entered college, I found encouragement, validation, and support from the brotherhood of my fraternity. I believe these were the reasons I turned out to be a decent guy in society. My mother played the biggest role in my life, being a single parent to my sister and me. She sacrificed her life so that we could have a better one.

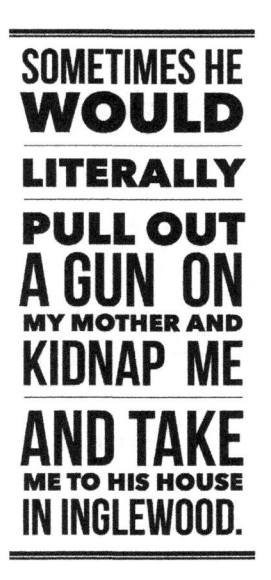

> **SOMETIMES HE WOULD LITERALLY PULL OUT A GUN ON MY MOTHER AND KIDNAP ME AND TAKE ME TO HIS HOUSE IN INGLEWOOD.**

Once I got married and had children, I found myself making a commitment to be the father that my father wasn't to me. I had to go to my Heavenly Father for guidance on how to be a good dad. I know it was the Spirit of the Lord who helped me become the best image of a loving father to my own children.

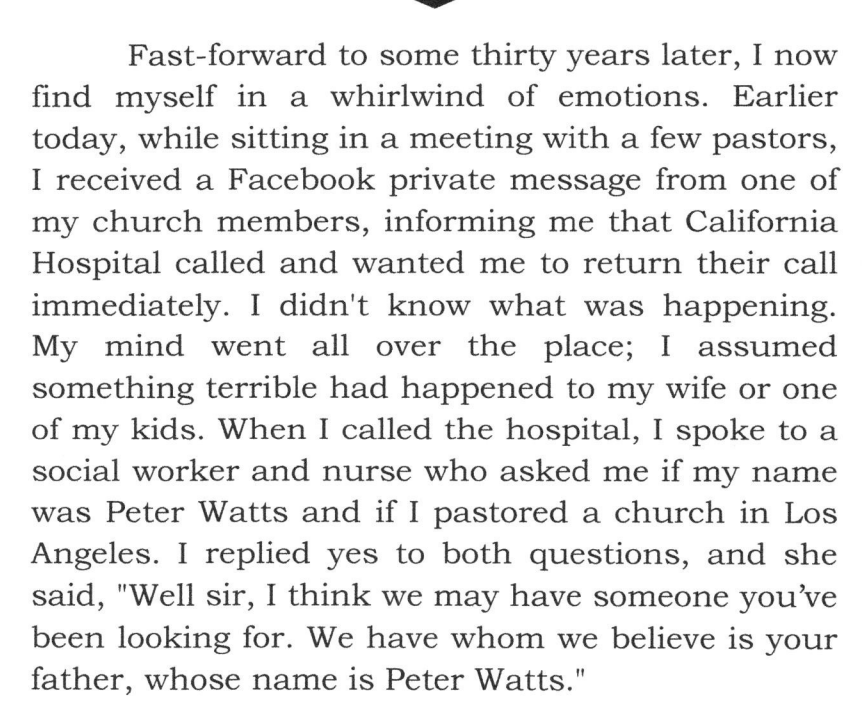

Fast-forward to some thirty years later, I now find myself in a whirlwind of emotions. Earlier today, while sitting in a meeting with a few pastors, I received a Facebook private message from one of my church members, informing me that California Hospital called and wanted me to return their call immediately. I didn't know what was happening. My mind went all over the place; I assumed something terrible had happened to my wife or one of my kids. When I called the hospital, I spoke to a social worker and nurse who asked me if my name was Peter Watts and if I pastored a church in Los Angeles. I replied yes to both questions, and she said, "Well sir, I think we may have someone you've been looking for. We have whom we believe is your father, whose name is Peter Watts."

I was floored! She continued and said, "We asked him if he had any next of kin. He said, 'I have a son that pastors a church in Los Angeles.'"

When my father told them that, the staff Googled my name to find my contact information and reached out to me. I was emotionally overwhelmed. I abruptly left my meeting, and scurried down the 110 Freeway to go see my father, Peter Watts, Sr. I had been looking for him for years, and now I would finally be able to see him. The last I heard, my father was living on Skid Row. About four months prior to the hospital calling me, I went to Skid Row to look for him, but did not find him.

I don't know what God will do with my experience of reuniting with my father, but I am willing to walk into the uncertainty of the future. The strange thing about all of this is that I don't care about what he did to my sister, my mother, and me in the past. I don't care about all the years he missed. I don't care about the Christmas gifts, birthdays, children's births, and graduations he missed. I don't care about the wedding he didn't get to attend. At this moment, all I want him to know is that I love him, and that God loves him even more.

> **DURING THESE FORMATIVE YEARS, IT WAS MY GRANDFATHER, UNCLES, AND FOOTBALL COACH WHO BECAME THE FATHER FIGURES I SO DESPERATELY NEEDED TO HELP ME MATURE.**

Chapter 5

MERCY

A lot has happened since I last wrote about my reunion with my dad. God's hand of reconciliation and redemption has been at work. I have seen God move on our behalf. I have been challenged to love, and show grace and mercy to a man who has not been in any part of my life for over thirty years. We are practically strangers to one another, but there is something so beautiful taking place in the midst of pain.

Since I found out my father was in the hospital, I have visited him each day. I was able to ask him questions and hear him talk about my childhood and things I didn't think he remembered.

Now, the real work has begun. I have received so many encouraging emails and phone calls, and they have strengthened me. I have also been in this place of the unknown. Sometimes people ask me what I'm going to do, and I quickly respond, "I don't know." I am on a true faith walk with God.

The hospital released my father to a recuperative care center, which happens to be ten minutes away from where I live. They fed him three hot meals a day and provided all of his necessities. He had a fourteen-day stay at this place. When the hospital gave me this information, I knew something had to be done after the fourteen days were up. Fortunately, Jennifer—a good friend of mine who runs a Skid Row ministry—reached out to help. Jennifer had heard about my father and sent me a text that read: "I know you have a hectic life, and I want to help you take care of your dad."

What?! I was floored by her generosity to help me navigate these unknown waters. Since then, Jennifer has helped me get my father a bed at the URM. The recuperative care center informed us that he would be assigned a caseworker who would help him secure permanent housing. The hospital workers helped him apply for a state identification card.

I can't express how incredibly thankful I am for the people God is using to help me with my dad. I have gone to visit him almost every day since he's been at the recuperative care center.

The first time I visited him at the center, I noticed he had about eight different prescription medications from the hospital. When he tried to take his medication, he accidentally spilled the pills all over the room. I found myself on my hands and knees picking up my father's pills from the floor, and trying to help him put them back in the bottle. In my mind, I prayed, *God please keep my heart soft toward him.* I graciously picked up the pills, gave him the dose he needed, and put the rest back in the bottle.

In a sense, I am tasked with being the parent to my father—the one who didn't fully raise me. There is no doubt that this has given me a new perspective and heart for the poor and marginalized in our society. I now have an actual face and connection to those who live in the streets and are disconnected from their families.

> I CAN'T EXPRESS HOW
> **INCREDIBLY THANKFUL I AM FOR THE PEOPLE GOD IS USING TO HELP ME WITH MY DAD.**

On the 22nd of May, my father will transfer to URM, where he will be assigned a caseworker who will help him get Section 8 and permanent housing. He will also receive mental health, medical, and dental services. I would not have ever imagined that being a pastor in Los Angeles, and a director at World Impact, would have remotely led to the reunion of my estranged father. I now understand what my grandfather meant when he would say that God works in mysterious ways!

My story is to be continued...

Chapter 6

BAGGAGE IN MARRIAGE

My daddy issues and father wounds have had a huge impact on my marriage. In times of uncertainty, my tendency to feel deserted, and like I had to prove myself to others, reared its head and caused much strife. 1997 marked our third year of marriage. We were going through a tough time deciding whether or not we would stay married or get divorced. By this time, we had two children, and we were both educators (I was in my first year of teaching). My wife was in a phase of not speaking to me, and her silence lasted a long time. Our conversations were few and far between—almost nonexistent.

One weekend, my wife left to attend an education conference in San Diego. When she came back, I could feel in my spirit that something was different, but I couldn't put my finger on what it was.

During Thanksgiving dinner, it all came crashing down. As usual, we attended a family dinner, but this time something was different about my wife. That day, she sat at the table unusually silent. I looked over to her and asked her what was wrong. She replied, "Nothing is wrong. I'm just thinking." I insisted we go out for a walk to talk, because something seemed off to me. As we walked down the street, I asked her again what was wrong. That's when she said it. "I don't think I love you. I think I married you for the wrong reasons."

Immediately, I assumed she was having an affair. On impulse, I said, "What's the guy's name!" In my mind, it *had* to be another guy. It couldn't possibly be that my wife was miserable in our marriage because of my possessive behavior. It couldn't be that we got married before we were mature enough to handle our problems (we got married when I was twenty-one years old).

The next three months would be a tumultuous time. We received counseling from our pastor. I remember one session when my wife was crying uncontrollably. My pastor said, "Look at her. Her heart is broken. You guys need to make a decision about what you are going to do."

We began having hard conversations about separating; we discussed child custody and how we would divide our material possessions. I often reflect back on this day, because it was when something in me began to rise up. It was when I finally recognized my insecurity and possessive behavior. Still, I had not realized that these behaviors stemmed from my father wounds. Even after my wife and I reconciled, I still battled with taunting thoughts that she might leave me. Every time there was an inkling of trouble in our marriage, my first thought was that I was being deserted. It wasn't until years later that I realized all of these feelings of abandonment came from my own father wounds. They came from my dad deserting his family when we were most vulnerable.

> **I REMEMBER ONE SESSION WHEN MY WIFE WAS CRYING UNCONTROLLABLY. MY PASTOR SAID, "LOOK AT HER. HER HEART IS BROKEN. YOU GUYS NEED TO MAKE A DECISION ABOUT WHAT YOU ARE GOING TO DO."**

Overtime, I was able to overcome my sense of insecurity by focusing on the promise of God that says, "I will never leave you nor forsake you." I had to plant that promise deep down in my spirit, so I would remember those words every time I felt deserted. Today, our marriage is the strongest it has ever been. When my wife and I reconciled, we agreed to never again bring up divorce. Since I began to process much of my past hurts from my father, I was able to improve the way I love my wife. We all bring emotional baggage from our past experiences into our relationships. Until we learn how to deal with baggage and not let it weigh us down, it will continue to present obstacles in the future.

Chapter 7

WHO'S YA DADDY?

Learning how to be a father when I was raised without one was like not having a manual for raising kids. I had to lean on a lot of prayer, discernment, and following the voice of God for guidance in making decisions concerning them. I remember when I first met my wife Didi, she already had a one-year-old daughter named Jasmin. Right off the bat, I knew if I wanted a relationship with Didi, I would have to take on the responsibility of fatherhood. I was twenty-one years old, and I didn't know what being a father was about. I never had a father.

My uncles and my football coach were my father figures. My fraternity group taught me a lot about being a man as well. Through them, I learned grit and how to overcome obstacles. I learned a lot about how to become successful in life, but there were no manuals for how to be a father. So, starting a relationship with someone who already had a child was daring and difficult.

At the time, my oldest daughter's biological father was still in the picture, but he wasn't actively involved in her life. It was difficult trying to navigate my relationship with my soon to be wife and my soon to be daughter.

Once we were married, we had an instant family. At twenty-one years old, I had to learn on the job. I thank God for His grace and mercy during that time; it was my reliance on Him that helped me be the father I never had.

There were times of disappointment. I think one of the hardest times we went through was during Jasmin's adolescent years, when she started middle school. She began to reject me as her father and rebel against our rules. As the man of the house, I had to enforce certain rules, but it was tough because there was this instant rejection that came from her. When I had to correct her, she would say things like, "You ain't my daddy. You can't tell me what to do."

There would be this embrace of her biological father that could have caused a lot of tension in our household, but I knew I had to respond with unconditional love. Although I was being rejected as the father, I still had to love my daughter like Christ loved me. One thing I made sure of was to never speak ill of her biological father.

Jasmin's father started becoming active in her life. Although I was the one raising her and taking care of her, she still yearned for her biological father. No matter how good children are loved by their father figures, they still want to be connected to their biological fathers in some way or another. Learning this truth helped me understand why there was this constant quest of finding my own father. In dealing with Jasmin, I had to let go of my own ego, frustrations, and how I thought things should be. I had to embrace the fact that she wanted a relationship with her biological father, and when I was able to do that, I was freed from the fear of losing my oldest daughter. I knew that our relationship was in God's hands and not mine.

Years later, I had my own son. Every father desires to have a boy. We named him Avery. One of the things I was certain about was that I would not be the type of father my father was to me. I was intentional about breaking generational curses when it came to fatherhood. I have always tried to be the best father to my children.

ALTHOUGH I WAS BEING REJECTED AS THE FATHER, I STILL HAD TO LOVE MY DAUGHTER LIKE CHRIST LOVED ME. ONE THING I MADE SURE OF WAS TO NEVER SPEAK ILL OF HER BIOLOGICAL FATHER.

When it came to my son, one difficulty I had was showing him affection and love outside of giving him things and doing things for him. I struggled with showing him authentic love.

I remember one time when Avery had gotten into trouble at school. I went to his room to chastise him. I remember saying to him, "I'm really upset about what you did, but I love you."

Avery started crying, and I asked him, "Why are you crying?"

He said, "Because you just told me that you loved me, and you never told me that before."

Now, I know I had told my son I loved him countless times, but for some reason, this was the first time he really heard those words come from me. It broke me to hear him say that. In that moment, I realized I was not good at expressing love to my kids. There needed to be this deeper authentic connection and demonstration of love, that had nothing to do with what I did for them or the gifts I gave them.

―――――◆―――――

I have a total of three children: two girls and a boy. My youngest child is my daughter, Imani. One of the things my wife and I have always tried to do was be positive examples for our kids, and I feel that we have succeeded in doing that. It was because of our village, and especially the men who helped raise me, that I was able to father my kids well. I was surrounded by good examples—older men who taught me a lot about being a man. I had my football coach, who taught me how to drive and taught me about the birds and bees. I had my grandfather who taught me about hard work and what it meant to love and protect a family. I had my uncles who helped hold me accountable for my actions when I was younger. My uncles were there to step in when my mother couldn't handle things with me. I took all the things I learned from these men, and used them as tools to be a great father to my own kids.

> IT WAS BECAUSE OF OUR VILLAGE, AND ESPECIALLY THE MEN WHO HELPED RAISE ME, THAT I WAS ABLE TO FATHER MY KIDS WELL. I WAS SURROUNDED BY GOOD EXAMPLES—OLDER MEN WHO TAUGHT ME A LOT ABOUT BEING A MAN.

This plays into the relationship we have with God. The relationships we have with our earthly fathers can sometimes be an indication of the relationship each of us has with our heavenly Father. When we have absent fathers—fathers we can't trust, or don't have authentic relationships with—it can be hard to trust in a God we cannot see. Just as our earthly fathers are absent, we feel that our invisible God in heaven is absent and untrustworthy. And so it takes the healthy relationships with fathers and father figures to help us develop an authentic relationship with our heavenly Father.

I'm sure Jesus learned how to be a man from his stepfather, Joseph. Imagine how Joseph felt being the father of God's son. Here you have a man who took in a wife, knowing she was pregnant with a baby who wasn't his. He took her in and married her so she would not be put to shame. He was responsible for protecting and providing for an instant family. Joseph was a carpenter. He taught Jesus his trade, and as a result Jesus became a carpenter too. I believed that's what the role of a father is: to take what you've learned and pass it down to your seed.

Lately, while spending time with my oldest daughter, who is now an adult, we've been able to reflect back on her childhood and how she perceived me as her dad. One difficulty that parents in blended families face is making sure all kids are loved the same. Stepchildren are known to feel like their stepparents treat them differently from their biological kids. That's something we as stepparents don't always think about. We don't always consider how the stepchild feels in a blended family. And as much as I tried to make Jasmin feel the same as her siblings, there were times when she felt like she

> **WHEN WE HAVE ABSENT FATHERS—FATHERS WE CAN'T TRUST, OR DON'T HAVE AUTHENTIC RELATIONSHIPS WITH—IT CAN BE HARD TO TRUST IN A GOD WE CANNOT SEE.**
>
> **JUST AS OUR EARTHLY FATHERS ARE ABSENT,** WE FEEL THAT OUR INVISIBLE GOD IN HEAVEN IS ABSENT AND UNTRUSTWORTHY.

had to work to get the same love and attention my biological children received.

When my oldest daughter felt like she wasn't getting enough attention, she rebelled. She acted out especially in middle school. Regardless of her behavior, it was incumbent upon me to really dig into developing a deep, authentic father-daughter relationship with her. Despite how I felt about her biological father, I was the one who chose to get into a relationship with someone who already had a child. This dynamic added more challenges to understanding what it meant to be a father. But at the same time, I was able to identify with Jasmin because of my own experience of not having a relationship with my biological father.

All of us need love from father figures, no matter how much we think we can do without them. When we are not connected to father figures, things get twisted and turned. When we don't have deep, authentic relationships with our fathers, hurt and dysfunction occurs in our lives. It's the reason why you see girls attaching themselves to guys who are no good for them. It's why guys attach themselves to other guys who are no good for them (e.g., gangs). These things happen when people are searching for deep and authentic relationships with father figures.

With my daughter Jasmin, I had to press in continuously and remind myself of the need for her to have a strong male presence in her life. I did not want her to go through the same things I had gone through. I remember when she was in a rebellious phase during her sixth grade year. She connected with these kids who were gothic, and she wanted to be goth. We would try to support her in all the ways we knew how. We bought her the black dickies, black nail polish, and black lipstick. We prayed for her, and tried to encourage her through this. It got to the point where some of the stuff she started doing was unhealthy and unproductive. We had to completely cut off all the gothic garb. As the man of the house, I had to step in and make that decision, knowing it wasn't going to be popular. I had to be a father to her, and not her friend.

Some fathers believe the best way to develop a relationship with their kids is to be friends with them on a platonic level. But our kids have enough friends. We are here to be their father figures. We should be their protectors and guides, who are able to give them wisdom on demand. We are to warn our kids about the potholes in life, so they don't have to experience what we went through.

My oldest daughter is now in her mid-twenties, and I appreciate how God used me to be a father figure in her life. We had lunch the other day and talked about her childhood. It was really encouraging to hear her say I was her father—not a stepfather, but her true father. She told me about a time when she was in high school and was having a conversation with her friend. While they talked, something in her clicked, and she realized I had always been there for her unconditionally, no matter what. When she looks back to all the times I had to be a disciplinarian, when I gave her advice, and when I protected and guided her; she sees evidence that I loved her unconditionally.

I believe our relationship grew because I was willing to step into those hard, uncomfortable places to show her a father's love. I didn't just give her stuff or do stuff for her; I showed her that I loved her for who she was.

In reflecting back from the beginning, from the time she was one-years-old and had her first boo-boo, I see how much my daughter has grown and how I was there to witness all of her accomplishments. I was there to see her culminate from elementary and middle school. I saw her graduate from high school. I saw her graduate with her undergraduate degree, and then her master's degree. I was there for every pivotal moment of her life. When she was in her darkest moments, I was there for her. Those are the things we cannot measure, buy, or even replace. Those are memories Jasmin will always have to carry with her throughout her life.

Chapter 8

TEACHER/PRINCIPAL/PASTOR/ FRIEND

I've had the opportunity to be a father figure to a host of young people through my ministry and educational career. I have always hoped my influence would be evident in the lives of the young people I've poured into. The apostle Paul spoke of this very idea:

> So neither he who plants nor he who waters is anything, but only God who gives the growth.
> (1 Corinthians 3:7)

I can't count on one hand how many teens I've had the opportunity to influence. Most are now young adults in college or in their careers. I'm not sure if helping them was a desire of my own or a way to make up for the absence of my father. On the one hand, I considered fathering others as a way to pay forward what my own father figures placed in me. After all, if it weren't for my grandfather, uncles, football coach, and fraternity brothers; I don't think I would be the man I am today. On the other hand, I worried that I was, in some ways, trying to earn the love of a father who didn't have the capacity to love me back.

When I was a youth pastor, my wife and I had the opportunity to work with kids all the time. We would go to their football games and cheer competitions, and also we would teach them about discipleship and what it meant to be a follower of Christ. A few of the young ladies in our youth ministry were a part of our church's step team. We treated these girls like they were our own children. When my wife and I had date nights, they would babysit our kids, and when they needed someone to represent them at back to school nights, I'd be there.

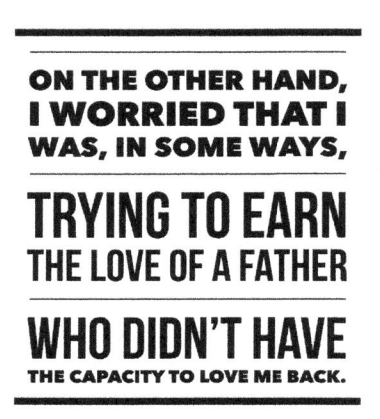

> **ON THE OTHER HAND, I WORRIED THAT I WAS, IN SOME WAYS, TRYING TO EARN THE LOVE OF A FATHER WHO DIDN'T HAVE THE CAPACITY TO LOVE ME BACK.**

This role of spiritual father was an important one I played, especially for young men in our youth ministry. I knew how it was to be an African American male raised in the inner city without a positive male role model. I knew the snares that waited to trap young black boys in the neighborhood. As a result, I felt the need to be a father figure to the young men who were drawn to me.

TEACHER/PRINCIPAL/PASTOR/FRIEND

When I became a teacher, my role as a father figure increased. I taught at a charter school that was predominantly African American, and most of the students came from families that were middle to upper class. Despite decent household income levels, many of our students were being raised without their fathers. When I taught third grade, I had a student whom I will call Cozy. Cozy was a great kid who had lost her father when she was in kindergarten. That year, I developed a strong bond with her family. I became a positive father figure in her life, which I believe helped her succeed in school. There were times, however, that I may have been there for Cozy and the rest of my students, to the detriment of my own children.

> **I KNEW HOW IT WAS TO BE AN AFRICAN AMERICAN MALE RAISED IN THE INNER CITY WITHOUT A POSITIVE MALE ROLE MODEL.**

Being a black male elementary schoolteacher is a rarity. When parents saw me along with my colleague Kenneth Wheeler—who is also a black male—they looked forward to having their kids in our classes. What happens, however, is that male teachers have unrealistic expectations on our roles as father figures, and we end up crippling our students by the way we overextend ourselves to protect them from the world. As parents, we can inadvertently bring about resentment in our households with our own children. There were times when I knew my own children felt shortchanged by the fact that I was spending the majority of my energy and time with other children rather than my own. My oldest daughter especially, who again is my step-daughter, felt left out because she thought I gave more attention to my students *and* my biological children than I gave to her.

There has to be a delicate balance between the time we spend with the children we serve and the time we spend with our own. Only God can give us wisdom in that area. The best-case scenario is when all of the kids feel like they are a part of one big supportive family, not just with me as the spiritual or biological father, but also with one another.

In 2008, I became the founding principal of a charter school in Los Angeles called Thurgood Marshall Leadership Academy. Here was the first time I would be in a leadership position, not just over a set number of kids contained in one classroom, but over an entire school community. Thurgood Marshall was unique in that we all felt like we were a part of one family. The teachers, staff, students, and parents knew there was something special about that school. To this day, I don't think I have ever experienced that kind of

TEACHER/PRINCIPAL/PASTOR/FRIEND

community, even at church or other organizations I've worked for in the past. My time at Thurgood Marshall was the biggest learning curve in my life's journey thus far.

I became close to a number of families who consequently joined our church family. Some families fell away for one reason or another. The greatest thing I learned in that season was to not overstep my bounds when it came to caring for families other than my own. I remember wanting those kids to have a positive male role model, and I so desperately wanted to help them get into college. My zeal destroyed long lasting relationships, because God's plans for those students were different from the plans I had for them. I didn't trust God enough to grow them Himself. I thought my own efforts were needed, and that I knew best as their *father figure*.

I can think of a couple of young people I fathered who are doing extremely well today. Brittney is one of them. Brittney was this firecracker student who had a mind of her own. She knew what she wanted and was very vocal about it.

We bumped heads often because she was strong willed and so was I. Brittney joined our church when she was in middle school. Every Sunday, we would pick her up along with about seven other kids, and we'd drive them to church with us. My SUV Tahoe was always packed with students from Thurgood Marshall. Recently, Brittney visited our church and talked about how she was so thankful for how my family encouraged her. She was finishing up her senior year at UC Davis and preparing to take the LSAT for Law School.

In the Spring of 2017, my wife and I flew to Tuskegee University to see another one of our young people name Chris, who had been a part of our youth ministry for years. He was graduating college and getting ready to enter graduate school. Chris and my son were best friends when they were younger, and they are still close to this day. When I think about how God orchestrated that relationship, it goes to show that He provides exactly what we need. My son, being the only boy in the family, needed peers his age to hang out with and develop positive relationships with. It was because I played the role of *father figure* to so many young people that my son got what he needed.

For me, the dark side of being a father figure is feeling the need to earn acceptance. In an unhealthy way, my effort to be a father figure was another form of *works righteousness*.[5] I was trying to earn something from a dad who never had the capacity to give me what I desperately wanted, which was acceptance and validation. In a sense, being a father figure to young people was my way of trying to gain self-worth; I wanted others to need me. Going down this path caused so many unhealthy behaviors to emerge. In my desire to be needed and accepted, I caused disruptions in families. I became overbearing. It took some time for me to realize my unhealthy behaviors, but thank God I wasn't too late.

It wasn't until I started to deal with my own fatherlessness that I began to see how my relationships were affected. I've learned that we can unknowingly create deep wounds in others while trying to help ourselves. These wounds can perpetuate the very problems we spend our whole lives trying to avoid.

When I started pastoring at The Rock Church, I began to see the importance of strong male role models in the community. Much of the ministry work I do is identifying, equipping, and empowering up and coming church planters and pastors in the community. Throughout church history, African American pastors have always been seen as the spiritual fathers of their communities or cities, and these giants in the faith have willingly taken on those roles. As a pastor, it is an honor to be recognized by your congregation and community every once and while. This is in no way meant to overlook the many black women pastors in our communities who function as spiritual mothers as well.

In light of the high rate of absent fathers in the home, I think that being an African American pastor is such a huge need for our community of young people. That's why when I talk to denominations, church planting organizations, and other networks about transitioning pastors out of their positions, I ask them to think carefully about how we do it in the context of African American communities. Having a pastor celebrate longevity in one church speaks to the fact that there are stable male role models who never leave their communities.

> IN A SENSE, BEING A FATHER FIGURE TO YOUNG PEOPLE WAS MY WAY OF TRYING TO GAIN SELF-WORTH; I WANTED OTHERS **TO NEED ME.**

Fatherlessness affects us all, whether we are pastors, educators, businessmen, or entrepreneurs established in our careers. I had an opportunity to speak at a Father's Day breakfast this past year. In my message, I talked about my relationship with my father, and the issues that I had gone through growing up. I shared some of the same information that is in this book. Afterwards, the pastor of the

TEACHER/PRINCIPAL/PASTOR/FRIEND

church came to me in tears. He was an older gentleman in his late fifties. He said he had never felt the courage to face or even deal with his fatherlessness until he had heard my story. Imagine that. Here is an older man leading a congregation to trust in the Heavenly Father, having never dealt with the issues he's had with his own earthly father. I imagine that this pastor's congregation, including the young people in his church, look to him as a father figure. It goes to show that God still uses us even in our brokenness, while we are yet on our own journey of healing.

Chapter 9

LETTER TO MY YOUNGER SELF

Hey Little Pete,

I just want to let you know how proud I am of you. Your life will become so much more than you could expect, and it's all because of God. I see the smile on your face in the picture with your mom, dad, and your younger sister. But it was at a time when no one could understand. You were confused when your mom and your younger sister had to flee in the darkest part of night, just to escape the abuse of your father.

I know it was difficult and you wondered what would become of you. If only you knew then that your upbringing is a part of your story and your journey as a leader.

You sometimes have nightmares from the times your father would come by your grandparent's house—high on drugs and out of his mind—because he wanted to see you. You would be afraid and wondered if he was going to kidnap you at gunpoint again, and take you away from your mother. You would hide in the bathroom and look out the window to see your grandfather wrestle with your father, trying to keep him from kidnapping you. Just know that those experiences will help make you a better father.

◆

Look at your smile, you little chocolate drop. You are black and beautiful, and as your grandmother would tell you: *God don't make mistakes.* During your elementary and high school years, you felt uncomfortable in your dark skin. Well guess what, little Pete? Your dark skin was kissed by nature's sun. Your dark skin is an oil field—precious and beautiful. I know the kids might have teased you and called you *tar-baby,* but those same kids will later come to realize that good black don't crack.

> I KNOW IT WAS DIFFICULT AND YOU WONDERED WHAT WOULD BECOME OF YOU. IF ONLY YOU KNEW THEN THAT YOUR UPBRINGING IS A PART OF YOUR STORY AND YOUR JOURNEY AS A LEADER.

◆

Look at you in college, finding the love of your life. Look at the beautiful children that will come from this union. Little Pete, you're going to be a fantastic father. You're going to be a fantastic

LETTER TO MY YOUNGER SELF

brother, a fantastic son, and a great husband. But even more than that, God is going to call you to be His mouthpiece as a preacher, speaker, minister, pastor, and even a charter school principal.

Yeah, that little kid who was overlooked because he was too small, not intelligent enough, and not vocal enough, will become one of the most prominent leaders of faith and social justice for the poor in the great city of Los Angeles.

The food stamps your mom collected is just another detail of your story, which will inspire and empower others who were raised in similar situations.

Little Pete, you don't know this now, but God is going to make you a servant to the city. You're going to be a great leader who leads young men and women in ministry. Little Pete, I'm so proud of you for not giving up and not listening to the naysayers. I'm proud that you didn't hold on to the negativity that was thrown your way. You could have given up when those editors told you that you couldn't write, when those teachers told you that you weren't smart enough, and when those people talked behind your back and said cruel things about you. I'm so proud you didn't give up, and you didn't listen to the negative noise. You stayed the course and believed in yourself, and you may not have known but there were others who believed in you too.

Little Pete, go and be everything God has called you to be, no matter what. Work hard so that when you are done, God can say, "Well done, good and faithful servant; you have been faithful over a few things, I will make you ruler over many things." (Matthew 25:23, NKJV)

Chapter 10

MAKE YOUR PAIN COUNT
Father's Day Sermon, 2016

Are they Hebrews? So am I. Are they Israelites? So am I. Are they Abraham's descendants? So am I. Are they servants of Christ? (I am out of my mind to talk like this.) I am more. I have worked much harder, been in prison more frequently, been flogged more severely, and been exposed to death again and again. Five times I received from the Jews the forty lashes minus one. Three times I was beaten with rods, once I was pelted with stones, three times I was shipwrecked, I spent a night and a day in the open sea, I have been constantly on the move. I have been in danger from rivers, in danger from bandits, in danger from my fellow Jews, in danger from Gentiles; in danger in the city, in danger in the country, in danger at sea; and in danger from false believers. I have labored and toiled and have often gone without sleep; I have known hunger and thirst and have often gone without food; I have been cold and naked. Besides everything else, I face daily the pressure of my concern for all the churches. Who is weak, and I do not feel weak? Who is led into sin, and I do not inwardly burn?

    If I must boast, I will boast of the things that show my weakness. The God and Father of the Lord Jesus, who is to be praised forever, knows that I am not lying. In Damascus the governor under King Aretas had the

PRODIGAL FATHER

city of the Damascenes guarded in order to arrest me. But I was lowered in a basket from a window in the wall and slipped through his hands. (2 Corinthians 11:22-33, NIV)

In making everyday count, we want to make sure that we maximize each day as if tomorrow is not coming. We don't know what the next day will bring, nor are we guaranteed to see it, but what we are sure of is that we can make our lives count for something in this present moment.

As fathers and father figures, we all want our lives to count for something. We all want to make an impact that goes far beyond ourselves, and even beyond our lifetime. At least for me, I want my life to count for something greater than me. I want my life to count, not only for my own benefit, but also for the benefit of my three children, my wife, and others important to me. Most importantly, I want my life to benefit the kingdom of God.

Today, I want to talk about something personal. I want to talk about making life count when it comes to being a father. I want to talk about pain. I know you might be thinking, *That isn't a Father's Day message. That's not what I was expecting to hear when I came to the Father Forever breakfast this morning.* But I want everyone to be aware that Father's Day is not joyful for everyone.

As a matter of fact, this holiday is a time of pain for those who don't have their dads with them to celebrate. This year is especially painful for our church, because my best friend and head elder is no longer with us. We suffered a great loss when he suddenly passed on December 1. As a church, we are still processing the pain of that loss.

This year is also unusual, because after thirty years of not knowing my dad and his whereabouts, I finally found him. I found him on Cinco de Mayo. I know the pain of finding and losing a father who has been in and out of my life. This is the first Father's Day weekend that I have been able to say I know my dad.

I hope this message will comfort your soul and encourage you to move forward with the plan God has for you.

Make your pain count! We all have dealt

> **AS FATHERS AND FATHER FIGURES, WE ALL WANT OUR LIVES TO COUNT FOR SOMETHING. WE ALL WANT TO MAKE AN IMPACT THAT GOES FAR BEYOND OURSELVES, AND EVEN BEYOND OUR LIFETIME.**

with pain at some point or another. The interesting thing about pain is, you never know when it will show up or when it will leave. Pain has a mind of its own. We tend to know when things like fear are approaching. Fear is an emotion we are used to, and is one that can typically be controlled. Fear is based on perception, which means that sometimes things appear bigger than they actually are. But *pain* is often unexpected and unfair.

Many times, we don't bring pain on ourselves, and we don't wish for it. It just finds us. And when pain finds us, it's hard to stay positive.

Many of you have experienced things that have cut you so deeply, that the wounds have yet to heal. I understand your pain, because I have them too. My father wounds are not something I enjoy bringing up in conversations. To be honest, I'd rather not relive any of the negative experiences I have had with my father. But I know that there is a God who can help us heal from our deep wounds.

Pain hurts and leaves behind scars that remind you of your experiences. Many of you have physical scars from your childhood, which are still visible today. When you see those scars, you are reminded of the pain and the situation that caused that pain. The same thing is true for emotional, psychological, and mental scars. These scars never go away until we deal with them. They continue to affect us until we surrender them to God.

How do we make our pain count?
Why do we run from pain?

When it comes to making our lives count as fathers and father figures, we must accept that

MAKE YOUR PAIN COUNT - *Father's Day Sermon, 2016*

pain is going to be a part of the process. If you have ever had a fitness trainer, you know that many often say, "No pain, no gain." In sports, athletes will often admit some type of pain they had to go through to reach victory. Pain is a great teacher if you are willing to endure the process.

In the 2016 NBA Finals, it was obvious that the Warriors were embarrassed after losing to the Cavaliers. They spent the entire year enduring that pain and allowing it to take them through the process all season until they won the finals the following year.

We all want our lives to count. We want to accomplish the dreams and plans that we believe God gave us. In 2 Corinthians 12, the Apostle Paul states that he wants his life to count, not because of his brilliance, but because of his weakness:

> But he said to me, "My grace is sufficient for you, for my power is made perfect in weakness." Therefore I will boast all the more gladly of my weaknesses, so that the power of Christ may rest upon me. (v. 9)

In this scripture, Paul states that the things that make his life count are not all of the good things he's known for, but instead the hardships he's had to endure with God's grace. He boasts in his pain rather than his pleasures, because in his pain he was able to experience the power of God.

There are two ways to view pain. We can either view it as punishment, or we can view it as pruning.

For many of us, pain feels like punishment. We ask ourselves things like: *God, why is this happening to me? Why am I dealing with pain again?* As fathers, we sometimes cry to God saying: *Why is my child not listening to me? Why is my job not fulfilling? Lord, what lessons are you trying to teach me? Why are you punishing me?*

> **THERE ARE TWO WAYS TO VIEW PAIN. WE CAN EITHER VIEW IT AS PUNISHMENT, OR WE CAN VIEW IT AS PRUNING.**

Many of us believe things happen to us, or pain visits us as a direct result of our actions. Those of us who were spanked as children were taught that pain meant punishment. Therefore, anytime we deal with pain in our lives, we tend to see it as a punishment from God. But I want to let you know that God is not punishing you. The pain you are experiencing is not because God is mad at you. It's not because he's trying to get even with you from the sin you committed. God is allowing pain to prune you.

I did some research to understand why gardeners pruned their crops. The research stated that the purpose of pruning was to open up crops for better air circulation, to encourage new growth and blooming, and to improve their shape. Making your pain count means dealing with the pain, in order for new growth to occur.

Even Jesus advocated the pruning process. In the gospel of John, when He talked about the true vine, He stated that we are the branches and God is the Gardener. In God's garden, there is a season of pruning. If we are going to make our pain count, we have to be willing to be pruned. Here is how God uses our pain to prune us:

1.) He knows when to prune us.
God knows the right season to begin the process of breaking away the hurt in your life. The pruning process does not happen when or how we want it to—and that's the painful part—but we must trust that God knows what's best for us.

2.) He uses the right pruning technique.
When pruning a plant, a gardener must use the right tool to cause growth, or else the plant will die. God knows how much we can bear. He makes sure that we can handle the measure of pain He allows. He picks the right trials and situations that will help us grow in Him.

3.) He prunes to maximize the health of the plant.
Pruning is when the gardener removes the dead branches off of a plant. In the same way, God prunes us by removing dead relationships, dead-end jobs, and dead-end situations that have no purpose in our lives.

Pruning for healthy growth is painful because sometimes we hold on tightly to things we think are good for us, when they actually hinder our growth. God has to literally pry us from that thing in order for new growth to happen.

In 2 Corinthians 12, Paul doesn't boast about his strength, he glories in his weakness. If he had a resume, pain would be listed as his qualifying strength．There's something about finding strength in weakness. There's something about admitting to God that we don't know the answers to everything. When we depend on Him, He supplies us with His wisdom. When we admit to God that we are weak, He supplies us with a strength we never thought was accessible. Paul explains the purpose for his pain this way:

> **THERE'S SOMETHING ABOUT FINDING STRENGTH IN WEAKNESS.**
>
> **THERE'S SOMETHING ABOUT ADMITTING TO GOD THAT WE DON'T KNOW THE ANSWERS TO EVERYTHING.**

> So to keep me from becoming conceited because of the surpassing greatness of the revelations, a thorn was given me in the flesh, a messenger of Satan to harass me, to keep me from becoming conceited. Three times I pleaded with the Lord about this, that it should leave me. But he said to me, "My grace is sufficient for you, for my power is made perfect in weakness." Therefore I will boast all the more gladly of my weaknesses, so that the power of Christ may rest upon me. For the sake of Christ, then, I am content with weaknesses,

insults, hardships, persecutions, and calamities. For when I am weak, then I am strong. (v. 7-10)

Paul had a pain in his side, and he couldn't get rid of it. He had a pain that God would not remove. Paul said his pain served as a reminder that He still needed God.

Some of us can relate to Paul and say that our pain is our weakness. Our pain remains there to remind us that we need God to handle it. He doesn't want us to bear pain on our own. He wants to remind us that we still need Him. When we recognize our weakness, then God becomes our strength. What do we do when the pain won't go away? How can we make it count for us?

1.) Know that God's grace is sufficient.
God's grace is there to carry us and hold us through the pain. If we are going to make our pain count, it can only count by God's grace.

2.) Continue to stand.
We may have cried all night long and thought about giving up on life, but we must stand anyhow. We may have attempted to do something and kept failing at it over and over again. The reminders of our failures are painful, but we should continue to stand.

The Bible makes clear that Christ endured pain just like we have to. There is nothing we have to go through that has not first been experienced by

Jesus. When we hold on to this truth, then we will be empowered to stand through our own pain. We should make our pain count, and not let the pain take us out for the count.

———◆———

At the time of writing this, I am in pain about my father once again. After he was released from the hospital, I took him to the Union Rescue Mission to secure shelter for him. That day, I sat by his side for four hours, waiting for a bed to become available. Once he had his bed, I told him I'd be coming back the next day to take him to the clinic to get a permanent doctor. The next day, I went back and he was gone. So, for Father's Day, I still have that pain—that thorn in my flesh—but it's just a reminder that I don't have to be strong. I don't have to endure this alone. I can glory in my weakness, and know that God will give me the strength to be the best father and father figure to the many people He brings in my life. I know that the grace of God has allowed me to be the father I never had to my children, and to literally break the curse and cycle of fatherless homes in my family tree. I know that the grace of God has helped me be a father figure to others and helped change the trajectory of their lives for the better.

Chapter 11

MY MOTHER'S PERSPECTIVE

Peter Sr. and I met when I was living on Main Street. I was in my second year of high school, and we met through mutual friends he lived with. We were introduced, and from there we started a relationship.

Originally, Peter lived in Louisiana. He left to stay with his brother Percy in Vegas. But then, Peter started giving Percy a hard time, and they had to call their older brother Sam. Sam came and got Peter from Vegas, and he brought him out here to California. Peter made neighborhood friends quickly and moved in with a roommate named Charles.

On the weekends, everybody would come over to Peter and Charles' apartment, which was pretty much the hang out spot. We would just hang out over there to party and have fun.

Peter was about six years older than me. He would always try to talk to me. At first, I was apprehensive, but later on I became impressed by him. He had that '54 Impala and was part of a car club called *Watts Up*. We started dating and eventually decided to become a couple.

Before my kids—Pete Jr. and Ebony—were born, Peter was a *go-getter*. He was always able to find good jobs. Once he would get tired or fired from one job, he'd find a new one in a matter of days. Peter always had money and would take me out and buy me things. He was a go-getter indeed, and very intelligent. While he worked, I went to school.

In front of my parents, he was very respectful. Raised with southern hospitality, he always answered with a, "Yes ma'am," or a "No ma'am."

We first lived on El Segundo, right off of Western in this apartment building called *The Sands*. Initially, Charles was Peter's roommate, but after I became pregnant with Pete Jr., Charles moved out and Peter moved me in. He told my parents that I was pregnant, and he said he wanted me to live with him. So, my parents gave us their blessing.

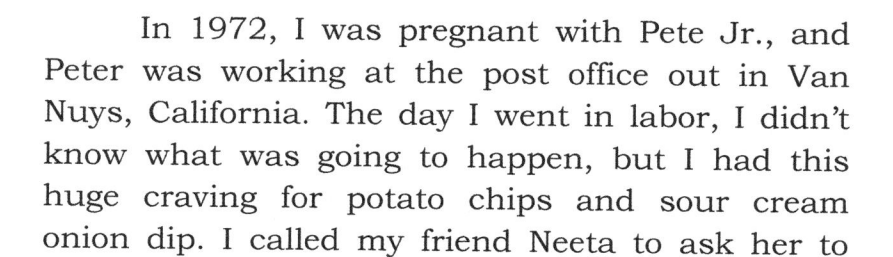

◆

In 1972, I was pregnant with Pete Jr., and Peter was working at the post office out in Van Nuys, California. The day I went in labor, I didn't know what was going to happen, but I had this huge craving for potato chips and sour cream onion dip. I called my friend Neeta to ask her to bring me something, because I had no car to get around. Neeta wasn't able to come, so I just went to bed.

That's when the labor pains started, but I didn't know what was going on. This was all brand new to me. I called Peter at work to let him know about the pain, and he said he'd try to get to me.

Then, I called Clara, a lady Peter used to stay with, who was knowledgeable about pregnancy. She got back in touch with Peter and notified him that based on my description of the pain, she believed I was in labor. She told him to come home right away.

I labored all night, because nobody was able to get to me. It was morning, around nine o' clock or so, when Peter and Clara got to me and took me to the hospital.

I found out why Peter's arrival was delayed. He had gone to Clara's house to work on his car because something was wrong with it. He couldn't get his car to work, so Clara took him to get me, and we rushed to California hospital.

Either the labor wasn't that bad, or I was too scared and distracted to realize the severity of the pain. I was in labor from about one o' clock a.m. until six forty-five a.m., when my son was born.
Peter had to leave the hospital to see about the car. I was there by myself for a while.

When my son was born, I could not hold him

or see him. The doctors had to rush him out because he was born with a murmur in his heart. The next day, after the doctors were able to get him stable, I was allowed to see him. The nurse took me to see my son in the incubator.

I completed my hospital stay as the doctors and nurses worked on the baby. When they discharged me from California Hospital, they transferred him over to Fountain Hospital (which is now just a medical clinic), right behind city college. He stayed there for two and a half months. I remember Peter and I would go to the hospital everyday to see the baby.

There was one trip I made to see him that I'll never forget. He had been there for about a good two months. I remember walking in the room to see my baby, but the incubator was empty. I screamed, "Oh my God! Nurse!"

The nurse came in and said, "Calm down. Don't worry. Your baby has graduated."

She took me to the room where my son was. Everything started falling in place with his health, but we still couldn't take him home until he reached five pounds. He was four pounds, six ounces; and it took him two weeks to reach five pounds. I remember Dr. Hines, who was the pediatrician, had to shave the baby's head, which made him look like a little Indian. Dr. Hines didn't know if they would have to perform surgery, so the baby's hair had to be removed just in case.

Finally, our baby reached five pounds, but we didn't have a crib yet. The doctor said it would be unsafe for the baby to sleep with us because he was so tiny, so I pulled out one of my dresser drawers, and I made the baby's bed by padding the insides with pillows and blankets. He fit right in it and slept in that drawer for a good week or so. And then, we got a crib for him.

The first house we purchased was in Inglewood. Peter and Charlie learned the roofing trade from my uncle, and they would get contracted to do roofing jobs. Along with that, Peter would do other side jobs and would get money from filing worker's compensation insurance claims. Peter would go to court to fight those companies, and he would win because he was a very believable person when he spoke.

Our family life started out really good. We hosted lots of house parties and backyard barbecues. Peter fixed up the garage and put out a red velvet couch. We had this huge barbecue grill and music system, and we'd entertain guests all the time.

All was well with our family, until Peter

started hanging out more with my cousin. I'm not saying my cousin was the cause of Peter's decline, because Peter was his own man, but this is when he started to change.

In the mid to late seventies, the black community experienced a big crack cocaine epidemic. Our family was not immune to that crisis. It started small—Peter and my cousin would bring kilos of marijuana to the house. They would break it down, bag it up, and prepare it to sell. I didn't know everything they were doing, and I didn't want to know; I just told Peter not to bring it in the house.

They started preparing the marijuana at someone else's house off of Broadway, back over in the twenties somewhere. That's when Peter started coming home later, and then he would not be home as much. He met other people who were into the same thing, and also he started a relationship with someone else. Then, he began to smoke sherm. At times, he would bring home the weed or a cigarette from the sherm, but this would not happen often because I asked him not to bring it in the house.

MY MOTHER'S PERSPECTIVE

When my son was six years old, I had my daughter Ebony. I thought another child would help our family, but it didn't. By that time, Peter and I were going through lots of problems because of what he was into. His head was totally messed up with the sherm; I didn't know he was smoking as much as he was. I started seeing lots of changes in him after Ebony was born. They could have been there all along, but I didn't recognize how bad off he was until Ebony was born.

> **IN THE MID TO LATE SEVENTIES, THE BLACK COMMUNITY EXPERIENCED A BIG CRACK COCAINE EPIDEMIC. OUR FAMILY WAS NOT IMMUNE TO THAT CRISIS.**

Peter never ran into trouble with the police due to drugs, but he did have problems with his job at the post office. He got caught heisting and taking packages. I remember when the detectives came knocking on my door to tell me that Peter had been arrested and that I needed to come down to the station. They interviewed me and asked me lots of questions. I found out that they were watching Peter at his job and finally caught him. But after the interview, they realized they didn't have much on him, so they released him.

Peter and I walked outside of the station, and I started to fuss at him. I said, "I told you, you can't be doing that kind of stuff and bringing it around me and my kids!" He shot back, "Shut up!" He did not want anyone at the station to hear me talk about his drug use.

I remember one night, my friend Charlesetta had come over to wash clothes. We were sitting at the table talking, and Peter was out in the garage. He came in the house and started opening and closing doors. Then he came in the living room where we were and just looked at us. He got on his knees and started to laugh and say, "Hahaha. I am God. I am God!"

> **I STARTED SEEING LOTS OF CHANGES IN HIM AFTER EBONY WAS BORN. THEY COULD HAVE BEEN THERE ALL ALONG, BUT I DIDN'T RECOGNIZE HOW BAD OFF HE WAS UNTIL EBONY WAS BORN.**

He scared us to death. Charlesetta called her husband, and he told us both to get out of the house. He said, "You know he's on drugs; you need to leave, because ain't no telling what he'll do."

Charlesetta left, and I walked the floor all night. After a while, Peter finally went to bed and slept until the next morning.

MY MOTHER'S PERSPECTIVE

I recall another incident that happened, right after Ebony was born. My friend Christine was at the house, and we were talking and eating fried chicken wings with lots of pepper on them. Ebony started crying, so I told Christine that I would be right back and took Ebony a bottle and tried to get her back to sleep.

All of a sudden, I heard this rumbling, and I put Ebony back in the bed. I walked toward the ruckus to see what was going on. Christine was leaving, and when I asked her what was wrong, she said, "You better tell that man of yours to leave me alone, because I will hurt him!"

She said that as she sat and waited for me to come back, Peter came behind her messing with her.

She said, "You better tell him something, because he don't know! I will take a knife and I will break him down like he was a side of beef."

Christine was a former butcher.

―――◆―――

I tried to leave Peter countless times. More than anything, I wanted to get my kids to safety, but whenever I tried to leave, Peter blocked it. He would lock the doors and stop me from leaving. I never stopped praying for God to give me the opportunity to escape.

One night, Peter came home and began to

turn on and off lights, open and close doors, and peer out of windows, claiming that the FBI was watching him. He went through these fantasies about being chased by the FBI and police officers. He picked up the phone and said it was bugged. He said that because we were near the racetrack and the Forum, people were looking for him.

I tried to reason with him and convince him that no one was watching him. Of course he wouldn't listen, so I sat at the table praying, and asking the Lord what to do. The Holy Spirit spoke to me and said to play along with Peter. I heard it as clear as day, and he said it again: *play along with him.* So I got up and started playing along with Peter's imaginations.

> **I NEVER STOPPED PRAYING FOR GOD TO GIVE ME THE OPPORTUNITY TO ESCAPE.**

When I saw him peep out the window and claim people were watching him, I said, "Oh, they sure are! My goodness! You know what? I think the kids and I should get out of here so you can handle what you need to with the FBI."

Then he said, "Yeah," and agreed with me. He grabbed a trash bag and started dumping the kids' clothes in it. I realized that this was my break away from him. He was moving us.

I called my dad, and he came with his truck.

MY MOTHER'S PERSPECTIVE

Peter helped us load the truck, and the kids and I went to go live with my parents at their house.

◆

A few days later, Peter started coming to my parents' house to try to get me to come back home. At first, he would come in his right mind and in a respectful manner. But then, he started calling me all the time, telling me to come back home. I would tell him no, and he'd say, "I kind of figured that."

One time, Peter came to my parents' house high on drugs. He was trying to take Pete Jr., and so I told Jr. to hide in the bathroom and to not come out until I told him so. Peter was so mad that we would not go back home with him that he slapped me. I pushed him back, and what saved him from going through the glass window were all of the unpacked boxes lying around. The boxes broke Peter's fall.

My dad heard the noise, and came and said, "Hey, what's going on with y'all?" He always tried to be the peacemaker. He tried to calm us down, but then I told him Peter hit me.

Then he said, "Boy, don't you put your hands on my daughter!" My father came between us to protect me, but Peter reached over him and hit me again. He hit me on the side of my head, and my daddy turned around and slapped him. That's when they started to wrestle.

They started wrestling from one room to the other. I ran to the kitchen and got a pancake spatula. I was trying to hit Peter on the back, but my daddy said, "Girl, move out the way!"

My daddy wrestled with Peter all throughout the house and ended up outside, because he was trying to push Peter out the house. I didn't know it then, but Pete Jr. was looking at the entire wrestling scene from the bathroom window.

THEN HE SAID, "BOY, DON'T YOU PUT YOUR HANDS ON MY DAUGHTER!"

My daddy was able to get Peter out of the house, and Peter left when he found out I called the police on him.

◆

One time, Peter came to my parents' house with a gun and took Pete Jr. I was so scared and didn't know what to do, but my dad tried to calm me down. He said, "Don't worry about him. He's going to bring him back. He can't take care of nobody." And my daddy was right; Peter brought Pete Jr. right back.

This wasn't the only time Peter threatened me with a gun. Before moving in with my parents, I once told him that I wanted to leave him, and he said, "You're not gonna leave me. You can't do nothing for yourself. You too stupid."

MY MOTHER'S PERSPECTIVE

I remember sitting on the bed while Peter was talking to me like this, and he said, "You think you gonna leave me? We'll see."

Peter pulled up the corner of the rug, and down at the floorboard he pulled out a gun and pointed it at me. He said, "If you leave me, I'll kill you."

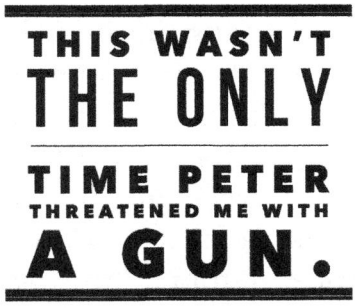

THIS WASN'T THE ONLY TIME PETER THREATENED ME WITH A GUN.

The Holy Spirit came over me, and all of a sudden I just jumped on the bed and said, "Go ahead! Shoot me! At least I'll be rid of you!"

Peter dropped the gun and said, "Girl, you crazy as hell." Then he'd leave me alone for a while.

Before Peter got really crazy, he would spend time with Pete Jr. He would do things like take him to the racetrack. We would go to church as a family, but Peter would never attend.

There was one incident that occurred while we were at church. I sang in the choir, and our church was invited to sing at another church, so while I went there, I had my parents watch Pete Jr. and Ebony until I returned.

When I was dropped off at my parents' house, Peter had Pete Jr. and Ebony in his car.

PRODIGAL FATHER

I had recently washed the laundry, and Peter had the nerve to have my basket full of fresh folded laundry I did in the middle seat of his car. Pete Jr. was sitting on the driver's side.

My dad was outside, calling out to Peter, "Hey boy, come back here! Bring them kids back here! What you doing?"

I jumped out the car and ran to try to get my kids. Peter asked, "Are you coming back home with me?" I told him I wasn't, and he told me that I would never be able to see my kids again.

I acted nonchalant about it only to trick him, and then I quickly opened the car door and snatched Pete Jr. and my laundry. Peter took off with Ebony in one hand, and he steered the wheel with the other hand.

I called the Inglewood police, and I remember a young black cop came out. I reported that Peter had kidnapped my daughter. The cop asked me, "Well, is that his child?" I admitted that it was. He said, "Well, you know, the law states that if the baby is his, he's not kidnapping."

I felt like I couldn't lie. I had to admit that Peter was the father. I didn't know then, but now I realize the cop was trying to get me to say Peter wasn't the father, so he could go out and get my child.

Peter kept Ebony for about a week. I would drive by his house to see what was going on, and

MY MOTHER'S PERSPECTIVE

sometimes I'd see Peter and Ebony outside. There were never any lights on. Ebony's hair was always sticking up and was never combed.

After a week, Peter brought Ebony back to me. I came home from running an errand, and found my dad holding Ebony in his arms. He said, "Peter dropped her off and said, 'Take her to the doctor. She got a cold.'" He brought her back to me because she was sick.

◆

During that time, the only thing that was going through my mind was that I hoped Peter would not break my kids' hearts, because I came to the conclusion that with or without drugs, this man was a liar. He was who he was, and he had been like that all of his life, even before the drugs. It's always been about what Peter wants, and never about sacrificing for his family. I prayed that the Lord would change Peter so my kids could get closure. I thought that maybe one day, Peter would be able to do right by Pete Jr. and Ebony, and would attempt to maintain some sort of relationship. But deep in my heart, I knew it wouldn't happen.

Chapter 12

FOR*GRIEVE*NESS

> Then Peter came up and said to him, "Lord, how often will my brother sin against me, and I forgive him? As many as seven times?"
> Jesus said to him, "I do not say to you seven times, but seventy-seven times." (Matthew 18:21-22)

The act of forgiveness, which Jesus demonstrated to his disciple Peter, is an act of continuous forgiving in the midst of this broken world. There are going to be times when we are in need of forgiveness, and there will be times when we'll need to forgive.

Forgiveness is one of the hardest practices for a follower of Christ. We think it's easy because the Lord commands us to forgive, but the actual act of forgiveness is very hard. We often think uttering the words, "I forgive you," settles everything and restores relationships back to normal, but this is a false belief. A father who abuses his child will never fully restore the relationship, even if he asks for forgiveness. That relationship will never go back to what it used to be. The father can be forgiven, but either the dichotomy of that relationship will change, or the very nature of it will change.

Miroslav Volf, the great theologian, talks about forgiveness in his book *Free of Charge*. After reading chapter six, "How Can We Forgive?" I felt challenged to consider my relationship with my father. In Volf's book, he states that forgiving is doubly hard because of the obstacle that "comes from the deeds that need to be forgiven." When we're receiving gifts, we stand empty-handed ready to receive the good graces of the giver. On the other hand, when we are the ones who need to forgive, we have a hard time because our offenders have burdened our bodies and souls with pain, and our injuries stand in the way of us being able to forgive. In other words, it's hard to forgive someone who has hurt us.

When we need to forgive, it's hard because we're holding in our hands the very thing that needs to be forgiven. We have a burden—this guilt or pain—we've carried throughout the years, because we've never forgiven our offender. What we must come to realize is that we don't have the power to remove moral guilt. Our hands are not even equipped to lift the burden of guilt or make the pain go away. Forgiveness is a supernatural act of God, and not of us. Yes, Christ has given us the authority to forgive, but it is only through God that forgiveness takes place. We are the conduits of forgiveness, and not the actual ones who forgive. When we recognize that Christ has forgiven us, it is easier for us to offer forgiveness.[6]

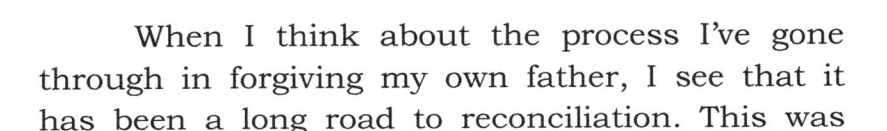

◆

When I think about the process I've gone through in forgiving my own father, I see that it has been a long road to reconciliation. This was not an overnight event. It was not some supernatural, *I saw him, I forgave him, and it is over and done with* event. Forgiveness is a process, especially when the offender is someone who does not have the capacity to receive forgiveness, or even acknowledge the one offering it.

> **WE ARE THE CONDUITS OF FORGIVENESS, AND NOT THE ACTUAL ONES WHO FORGIVE.**

Now, I know you're reading this and you're thinking, *wait, he should have been asking **you** for forgiveness for what he did to you and your family.* But that's where I want to challenge those of you who are reading this book. Many times, we are unable to release the pain from someone who has offended us, because they are unable to offer us forgiveness, and so we hold on to that pain for the rest of our lives.

One thing that makes this whole idea of forgiveness difficult is that as forgivers, we feel pressured to make it happen instantly. We are taught that we have to forgive our offenders right away. But true, authentic forgiveness does not work like that. When we think about the Lord's Prayer, we're often held hostage to the line that states, "but if you do not forgive others their trespasses, neither will your Father forgive your trespasses" (Matthew 6:15). In some way, we have perverted that text to believe that we have to earn our forgiveness by *doing* something. And we know that grace isn't about earning anything; it's about receiving something you don't deserve. So essentially, our forgiving becomes this work we're doing to try to earn a release of guilt or a release of the burden in our lives. But forgiveness is taking time to work through whatever hurt, injury, or pain we have experienced in order to regain that relationship with our brother, sister, father, mother, or companion—whomever it may be.

So when we look at forgiveness and we look at reconciliation and justice, all of those words are not individual concepts, but they are all wrapped up in the same thing. My forgiveness *is* my reconciliation, and it *is* my justice. So, when we talk about forgiveness, we're talking about the process of healing. With my father, it has been a process of healing and not an overnight activity. In this process, I'm learning about myself, as I wrestle with the fact that I found my father and had a season of being with him and learning more about who he is, who I am, and why my childhood was the way it was. There have been times when I wanted to simply deny my father forgiveness, because of the sickness he carries from his drug addiction. When someone has abused drugs for as long as my father has, it is not something they just want to do, but it becomes something they feel they *have* to do, because their bodies have become so dependent on it, thus making it an illness. I thought that after my father got to see his own flesh and blood after thirty years, he would have been willing to step away from the destructive life he lived. I thought he would have pulled away from drugs when he saw his son and daughter, and when he knew he had grandchildren. I thought he would have been able to muster up the strength to pull away from the streets when he saw that there was a family waiting to receive him and support him. But because his drug dependency is a sickness, he fell right back into the trap of drugs after reconnecting with us.

> **WITH MY FATHER, IT HAS BEEN A PROCESS OF HEALING AND NOT AN OVERNIGHT ACTIVITY.**

◆

I remember taking a class at Fuller Seminary on the practice of community, and we had to read this interview called *The F Word*. In that interview, *the f word* discussed was *forgiveness.*

This question was asked: *When it comes to forgiveness, does the appropriate response change if what we receive is an account of what had happened or what was wrong, or an appeasement rather than an apology?* I remember reading this interview, and the answer suggested was, if the person has offered you an appeasement, you can say, "Come, let's talk about what really took place between us, without either of us competing as to who was truly at fault."

From this, hopefully a true apology would come about, but if the person continues to offer only an account, then the most the forgiver can do is *grieve.*

The interviewer stated that it is common for an apology to not come about from a person in recovery. And so the question becomes: *What if you want to forgive someone, but that person is emotionally unavailable, or they don't acknowledge the injury they have caused you, or the person has died?* In such cases, the best thing to do is *grieve,* and that's why I titled this chapter *Forgrieveness* instead of Forgiveness. The process of *forgrieving* is just like grieving and processing the loss of a loved one. The stages of *forgrieving* are similar to the stages in the grieving process.

In the process of *forgrieving,* there is this shock, and then there's numbness. Then, there is the stage of allowing yourself to move from guilt to anger, and then all of a sudden this anger goes away and you move into the stage of acceptance. If you've ever lost someone close to you, then you understand the stages of grief I've just mentioned. The grieving process can be so grueling to where you're just ready for it to pass, but you realize it will not go away, so you just ask God to help you through it.

Going through the process of *forgrieving* my own father has helped me get to a place of healing and restoration. Initially, I was in shock when I saw him after thirty years. I couldn't believe it, and I felt like it was a miracle that we reconnected. Then, I felt numb. I began to recount and remember all of the things that happened as a result of him not being there to raise me. I thought about all the injuries he caused my mother and my sister, and all of the things that came about because of what he put us through.

This led me to feel angry. You'd think I'd be overjoyed to reunite with my father—and I was— but after a while I just felt angry. I was angry at the fact that he couldn't change, as much as he wanted to. I was angry that I couldn't make him change. Because I was angry, and I knew it wasn't his fault, I began to feel guilty about my own anger. I had to accept the fact that at this point of my father's life, he was not going to change or be different. I asked God to help me accept this fact, and after a while I was able to release my anger, shame, and guilt to Him. It was too heavy for me to carry that burden.

> Come to me, all who labor and are heavy laden, and I will give you rest. (Matthew 11:28)

I found myself resting in the hands of God. I turned over my anger and guilt about my father into the hands of my heavenly Father, and I trust that God will carry this burden for me for eternity.

Am I a better person than I was yesterday? Absolutely. Am I growing continually? Absolutely. Will I ever be the same? Absolutely *not*. So, for those of you who are reading this book, I pray that you will allow yourself to go through the process of *forgrieving,* in order to reconcile with your own fathers. At the end of the day, it's about forgiving those who have hurt us, because Christ has forgiven us.

Notes

Introduction

1. Source: *Family Structure and Children's Living Arrangements 2012.* Current Population Report. U.S. Census Bureau July 1, 2012.

Chapter 1

2. The acronym *TUMI* stands for *The Urban Ministry Institute. TUMI* is the national training arm of World Impact, and "equips leadership for the urban church, especially among the poor, in order to advance the Kingdom of God." Source: *The Urban Ministry Institute (TUMI).* "Transforming Inner Cities." http://worldimpact.org/our-ministry/the-urban-ministry-institute.

3. The SIAFU Network "is a national association of chapters anchored in local urban churches and ministries designed to identify, equip, and release spiritually qualified servant leaders to reach and transform the poorest unreached communities in urban America." Source: *The Urban Ministry Institute (TUMI).* "Transforming Inner Cities." http://worldimpact.org/our-ministry/the-urban-ministry-institute.

NOTES

Chapter 4

4. The term *sherm,* also known as phencyclidine, is "an animal tranquilizer smoked as a narcotic." 2007. http://www.dictionary.com/browse/sherm.

Chapter 8

5. According to The Institute For Faith, Work, & Economics, the term *works righteousness* "is a form of self-righteousness that believes that our salvation can be earned and/or sustained by doing good works. It says we can make ourselves righteous before God by our obedience." February 9, 2015. https://tifwe.org/faith-and-work-vs-works-righteousness.

Chapter 12

6. See Miroslav Volf, *Free Of Charge,* (Grand Rapids: Zondervan, 2009), 193.

Made in the USA
Middletown, DE
21 April 2021